Mason Bees
for the Backyard Gardener

INKWATER
PRESS

PORTLAND • OREGON
INKWATERPRESS.COM

Sherian A. Wright

ISBN-13 978-1-59299-461-8
ISBN-10 1-59299-461-X

Publisher: Inkwater Press

Printed in the U.S.A.
All paper is acid free and meets all ANSI standards for archival quality paper.

1 3 5 7 9 10 8 6 4 2

Contents

Preface

· ·

This is a practical guide for the everyday gardener who would like to do something extra special for their garden. I wish to draw particular attention to the fact that fruit trees can produce more fruit with very little effort. This book will introduce you to the best pollinator around - the Mason bee. In fact this little bee could be in your garden right now. All it needs is a home - a nesting box.

This book is a reference guide written in a simplified and usable format. My application is strictly for the backyard gardener who, not only wants more fruit from their trees, but wants to provide a habitat for our native Mason bee. Using this guide makes it easy to get started "beekeeping" Mason bees.

With the serious issues regarding the decline of honey bees, I see this little Mason bee gaining in popularity; and I want to take part in giving this native bee the recognition that it deserves.

My ultimate goal is to excite people in such a way that they become proactive in the preservation of this very important second-source pollinator.

Biography

I've been studying and documenting the Mason bee's life style for about 8 years. My past experience as a mechanical design engineer for prototype projects, influences by approach in compiling information for release to the general public. I prefer to find a common ground with folks so that we can share and learn from each other.

I've created Mason bee-specific presentations for garden clubs, master gardener's training sessions, schools, nurseries, environmental groups and related college classes. I continue to work on various experiments of my own to either prove or disprove some of the information that is being published. I maintain a nature diary, noting weather conditions and bee activity. I keep a record of the trees, flowers and plants that are blooming during the "bee" season. Climates can vary within a 2 mile radius, and I try to make people aware of their own personal micro-climate and to pay particular attention to their fruit tree's blooming cycle.

I'm am an enthusiastic gardener/naturalist with a desire to learn all I can about what's happening in my immediate environment. My encounter with the Mason bee left such an impression on me that I just had to share my findings with others. I put together this guide to not only make people aware of this bee's existence, but to give them the opportunity to provide a desirable habitat for this very important northwest native.

Acknowledgments

· ·

I offer my sincere thanks and graditude to my wonderful and patient husband, Malcolm, who provided technical help in using software to layout my book and for his continued support in all my endeavors by assisting me in presentations to various groups, organizations and institutions. His positive encouragement has motivated me to put together my collection of information and experience for others who would like to become involved in the simple process of Mason "beekeeping."

I also have to thank many friends, relatives and strangers who listened to me talk about Mason bees every time I discovered or uncovered some bee fact that I just had to share.

CHAPTER 1

Getting Started

· ·

This chapter will highlight some of the key features of the Mason bee and some of its requirements along with questions that are generally asked about its benefits and usefulness. In other words, this is a jump start or an outline of things to come in the following chapters.

Figure 1.1 - Female Mason bee

What do Mason Bees look like?

The Mason bee is a real bee but at first glance, the female in particular, looks somewhat like a garbage fly. *Figure 1.1* is a good example of this mistaken identity. In my area I have found the female to vary in size, sometimes smaller than a honeybee and other times a little larger. However, the male overall is always smaller than the female, has longer antennae and more white facial hair - see *Figure 1.2*. He's just a real cute little fellar out to woo the ladies. Basically, our northwest native bees are an iridescent blue-black color and have four wings; the fly, on the other hand, has only two wings, but we'll cover more descriptive comparisons in **Chapter 3 - Bee Profile**.

Figure 1.2 - Male Mason bee

What's in a name?

The term "Mason" is an analogy to the female's skills in creating mud walls for her cells or chambers. She layers little pellets of mud, much like that of a bricklayer; hence living up to her title. This bee is also referred to as an Orchard bee, a Blue Orchard Bee (BOB) and of course its scientific name (*Osmia lignaria*), narrows the region to the northwest and British Columbia areas. There are other Osmias throughout the United States and Europe, but my focus is specifically on our local bee. Throughout this guide I will use the name "Mason bee" - as it is the most commonly used term for this solitary bee.

What are Mason Bees good for?

The most important thing about the Mason bee is her pollination skills. If you have fruit or nut trees or even berries, then this is definitely the bee for you. See **Chapter 4 - Pollination**.

What do Mason Bees need?

- Housing Units and Shelter with 5/16-inch holes
- Mud
- Flowers
- Temperatures 55°F - 60°F to get started

Where are they?

Mason bees are found all over the world and may be in your own backyard. In their zeal to get started, the bees have the ability to seek out nesting sites on their own - under roof eaves, in window casings, patio umbrellas, wind chimes and even recessed screw holes. This creative little bee has even used the folds of material in an armrest on an outdoor swing while I was sitting in it. I cannot help but admire her ingenuity. This bee does not excavate or create holes of any type. She uses **existing** holes - and that's where we, as individuals, can assist her in her endeavors to create a home for her future children.

What kind of tools do I need?

The beauty of "keeping" Mason bees is that no special equipment is needed.

How many bees do I need?

The average urban garden will find that one housing unit of 25 holes or straws, will be sufficient to pollinate their fruit trees.

On the other hand, if you have an acre of fruit trees, then you will need about 250-300 female bees. You can figure that you'll have about one or two females per hole or nesting straw. Again, if you only have a few fruit trees, a nesting unit of 25 holes or straws will be more than adequate to meet your pollinating needs.

Can I reuse the Nesting block or straws?

For the second year it is a good idea to have another unit for emerging bees to use. However, on a personal note, even though I've provided new housing units, some of the bees still prefer to clean out the old home site and reclaim it for their future offspring.

When do Mason Bees emerge?

In the early spring (late March or the beginning of April)when temperatures start to warm up and stabilize around 55°F - 60°F for a few days, the males will start to emerge first. Here in the northwest, this warming trend usually occurs at the end of March or the first part of April; of course, there are always exceptions to the norm. I've seen cold weather stay through May resulting in Mason bees emerging **after** the fruit trees' blooming cycle - the end result being very little fruit in the fall. If temperatures drop after the emergence, the males just hang around in the holes and wait until things warm up. The females come into view a few days after the males. Again, their appearance also depends on the same temperatures.

How does the pollination process begin?

When the male first emerges, he poops *(Figure 1.3)* and then looks for the closest flower to imbibe in a little nectar. All he needs is enough sustenance to mate with the female. To facilitate this need, I have an Andromeda *(pieris japonica)* growing nearby. It is usually blooming early and provides a much needed food source on a continuous basis, supplementing the between times of fruit blossoms. The male may do some pollinating during his short life (about 2 weeks), but it's the female Mason bee that is receive full credit in pollinating the fruit trees, nut trees and berries that are blossoming in early spring. See **Chapter 4 - Pollination** and **Chapter 6 - Food Sources**.

Figure 1.3 - Bee Poop

Where does the bee get mud?

All that the Mason Bee needs for her construction project is a hole and some mud. I've personally tried to provide a dish of mud near the nesting site, only to find that my good intentions were totally ignored. The bee searches for a wet clay mineral-type soil, but she alone determines the wetness-gauge by digging down to a consistency that suits her requirements. She has an amazing ability to determine the moisture and mineral content of the soil needed to form the wall for the cell.

On our property we're fortunate enough to have a wetland and a hillside with numerous underground and surface springs that keep certain areas consistently wet - and our bees have discovered these sources on their own.

If you do not have such a site, you can create a moist patch of soil in your yard near the nesting site. See **Chapter 5 - Housing**, "Creating a Mud Reserve," for more information on this project.

How do I "keep" Mason bees?

There are several options for "keeping" Mason bees.

1. Nesting boxes can be left in place, but need to be in a protected area such as under the eaves of a roof, workshop, balcony, etc. Some nesting boxes have small roofs, but there may not be enough overhang to protect the unit from rain, especially when there is a rain-wind combination.

2. The trend now is to use tubes or liners/straws. These items may help combat mites but other problems can still occur. I will discuss some of these issues in **Chapter 9 - Enemies**. Once a tube or straw has its final mud plug, it can be collected and stored in a waterproof container with a lid. Do not store in a room that might reach or exceed temperatures of 50°F or you will have bees emerge sooner than expected. The goal is to protect the tubes from moisture and predators.

3. In late September or early October, the cocoons can be harvested and then stored for the

March emergence. See **Chapter 8 - Winterizing Bees.** This method of storing bees is not mandatory, but is interesting to try. You'll definitely see how many good cocoons you'll have for the coming spring.

4. Build and they will come; however...You can purchase housing units and supplies at some nurseries, feed stores or bird shops as well as online.

5. When it comes to ordering bees, it is recommended that you order or check with your local bird shop or nursery as early as possible, usually by the first of January. They may still have bees in February, but any later than that you'll be out of luck. The bees are are sold by the tube (the number of bees in a tube can vary), or by a vial or unit of cocoons.

> **Hint**: The terms "straws" or "liners" are used interchangeably throughout this guide; a tube, on the other hand, is reference to cardboard material of 4 mil thickness.

Anyone can "keep" these bees. Building your own nesting unit is not hard to do. *Figure 1.4* depicts one of my setups to observe Mason bees. You can see my various nesting options; I've used everything from a typical Mason Bee block to a wooden knife holder. At night I use a flashlight to peek in the holes and count how many bees I have; their iridescent bodies reflect the light which makes it very easy for me to see them.

Will the Mason bees stay on my property?

Once you have the bees, they will basically be yours and stay on your premises. This bee does not care to travel long distances (her range is usually no more than 300 feet from the nest).

Figure 1.4 - Balcony Retreat

CHAPTER 2

Bee History

• •

I*n the beginning...* it was all about the honeybee. Their precious gold (honey) has always been given high recognition, not only today, but dating back to the pyramids of Egypt. Along with the bumblebee, these bees are the ones most noticed gathering nectar and pollen from flowers in the garden. We might observe other little bees and bee-like insects, but they do not dominate our thoughts or concerns.

The honeybees are actually not native to our country; they were brought to North America by the Pilgrims about 1621. They were originally imported from Europe but became accepted as true "Americans" over time because of their contribution to pollinating crops and providing honey. The honeybee populations became divided between wild bees and the well-known domesticated bees. With the advent of development and pesticides, approximately 90% of our wild bee populations have been destroyed. Domesticated bees are also losing ground and many commercial beekeepers are having difficulty maintaining enough hives for the farmers.

Now lets take a look at one of our own native bees - Osmia Lignaria - also known as the blue orchard bee or the Mason bee. I prefer the name "Mason bee" as it is simple and easy to remember and serves as an excellent descriptor of the bee. The vast majority of native bees are the solitary types, and our Mason bee is part of this group.

Mason bees are found throughout the world. One of the first studies of this bee was made in France by Rene' Antoine Ferchault de Reaumur (1683-1757). His report on the story of the Chalicodoma of the Walls, whom he called the Mason-bee, served as a springboard for a book written by J. Henri Fabre (1823-1915). Henri did not recognize Reaumur's method of documenting the Mason bee as meeting scientific criteria. However, Fabre' was able to glean enough information from Reaumur's papers and pursue experiments on his own to put together his book, "The Mason-Bees." This book documents his personal adventures and various experiments with these bees. During his lifetime he studied and documented various insects and spiders and became known as the father of modern entomology. "The Mason-Bees" was originally published in French in 1914 and then translated into English in 1916 by Alexander Teixeira De Mattos.

CHAPTER 3

Bee Profile

· ·

This chapter profiles the Mason bee by defining basic characteristics and anatomy. In reviewing bee societies there are two major groups: the social bees and the solitary bees.

The Social Bees

Before we get into Mason bee specifics let's take a look at the social bee kingdom. Most people are familiar with this group of bees (i.e. honeybees and bumblebees - see *Figure 3.1 & Figure 3.2*). Their family structure consists of workers, drones and a queen; the division of labor all comes together to serve and nurture a single queen bee. The honeybees raise, protect, feed, and cool the hive as necessary. Social bees work together in an extremely organized and complex manner for the greater good of the colony.

Figure 3.1 - Honeybee

Figure 3.2 - Bumblebee

The Solitary Bee

A solitary bee, on the other hand, takes on all the responsibility of creating a life support system for each egg that she lays. She is a queen and worker bee, all in one - a single working mom by today's standards.

Some of her cousins include leafcutter bees, carpenter bees and some wasps.

In general, the solitary bee gathers nectar and pollen (this mixture becomes bee bread), puts it in an available hole or cavity, lays an egg in the bee bread, leaves some space for the larva to grow and makes a partition of some natural materials (mud, gravel, leaves, etc.) to divide the egg cells from one another. She basically operates in a set-it-and-forget-it mode. Her nonaggressive behavior might relate to the fact that she does not feel the need to protect her egg because, as far as she's concerned, her offspring are sealed and protected in their chambers.

Being solitary does not mean that the bee dwells alone in some remote location. On the contrary, they all get along quite well and will often reside in the same nesting unit without intruding on each other's nesting cavities. Each female designs and constructs a special life-support system for each egg and uses her own special perfume (pheromone) to mark her homesite. I find it most interesting that her body features a special sac for storing sperm, and she can release the sperm at will if she decides it's time to have a girl. The girls are produced only from fertilized eggs; the unfertilized eggs become boys. The female eggs, which are most coveted, are usually placed at the back of the nesting tube. One theory is that it offers them more protection from outside invaders, and there are plenty of males that can be sacrificed up front.

The hole depth will determine how many female eggs will be laid. An average estimate is approximately 2 females, 4 males per 6-inch length. Providing a longer length, however, will not guarantee any more females. I have found tubes with lots of space between cell chambers with only two or three cocoons in the entire length of the tube. The bees don't always fill to capacity. Sometimes an entire tube will have only male bees. The bee herself is the only one who knows the reason why.

Taxonomy of the Mason Bee

Here's a partial taxonomy of our Mason bee:
- **Class:** *Insecta linnaeus* (insects)
  - **Order:** *Hymenoptera linnaeus* (ants, bees and wasps)
    - **Family:** *Megachilidae*
      - **Genus:** *Osmia*
        - **Specific name:** *lignaria*
          - **Scientific name:** *Osmia lignaria*

The Osmia lignaria by any other name is
- Blue Orchard Bee (B.O.B)
- Orchard Bee
- Orchard Mason Bee
- Mason Bee

Mistaken Identity

At first glance, this bee looks like a garbage fly and by default this becomes part of her description. The green or blue-black iridescent body is indeed strikingly similar, but from that point on, there are basic bee-fly body differences. In *Figure 3.3*, I have simplified the key features that set the two apart. An example of one difference is that the wing formation of a garbage fly has a delta shape, extending out on each side of the body. The bee's wings, on the other hand, lay back flat and parallel with the body, crossing at the tips when she is exploring a flower.

The female bee has some additional features that include antennae and a stinger. Her stout body - she's a full-figured bee - is covered with a lot of hair. She also has a surprisingly long tongue which she keeps curled along side one cheek when not in use.

People have seen this little bee come out from under their roof shingles and immediately assume that damage is occuring when, in reality, it becomes a

Figure 3.3
Bee-Fly Comparison

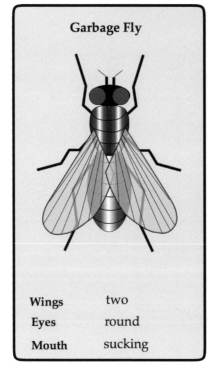

Garbage Fly

Wings	two
Eyes	round
Mouth	sucking

Mason Bee

Wings	four
Eyes	oval
Mouth	mandibles

victim of circumstances by using preexisting holes. In reality, the hole could have be vacated by a Carpenter bee who is usually the one responsible for making holes in wood, especially in houses. This bee is black, but is basically hairless and much larger. The bottom line is that the Mason bee in her quest to find a suitable cavity for her egg, explores all possibilities and uses only **existing** holes

The Fly that Looks Like a Bee

Now that we've covered the bee that looks like a fly, how about a fly that looks like a bee? There's a bee-type fly that actually looks and behaves like a bee. It pollinates and has a similar wing profile, but the same basic differences still apply: number of wings, eye shape and mouth parts.

One example of such a fly is the Hover fly, alias the " flower fly" (*Figure 3.4*). This fly is found pollinating flowers in early spring; and like their name suggests, they hover about much like a little helicopter. I've recorded their activity on plum tree blossoms in early spring. They were out and about just before my Mason bees had emerged.

Figure 3.4 - Hover Fly

Attitude/Sting Behavior

When I talk about the Mason bees, one of the first questions asked is "Do they sting?" In any bee family structure, the female is the only that has this feature. It's all part of her ovipositor; in fact you might call it the finishing touch. Female Mason bees are equipped to sting, but are not inclined to do so unless provoked. I, personally, have not tried to squeeze the bee to test her stinging power, but I have talked with a couple of farmers who purposely squeezed her. I was informed that the infliction could be compared to that of being a little greater than a mosquito bite. This bee does not lose her stinger and has the ability, like a wasp, to sting repeatedly until she delivers her message.

All in all, this bee is typically nonaggressive. The behavior pattern may be attributed to the fact that she doesn't have a large hive infrastructure to protect. Working singly does seems to be the reason for the mild-manner behavior. Once her egg is set in the bee bread and the cell sealed, there is no compulsory need to defend. The honeybee, on the other hand, works as part of an organized community to protect the hive (nest) and the queen.

The bees tend to ignore me when I'm watching and photographing them. I've let first-emerged males crawl on my finger. They do a series of preflight tasks, stretching hind legs, checking their antennae shaking their behinds. In fact they're so comfortable in my presence that they relieve themselves on me just before takeoff.

Later, after the females merge, they will buzz around my head, checking my nose and ears as possible nesting sites. On one occasion the bees were claiming their nesting holes while I was drilling out a block of wood. They paid no attention to the noise and activity. I would no sooner drill a hole, than a bee was crawling inside and claiming it as her own. I almost think that the sound of my drill brings them in. On a personal note I can drill 50 holes before by 9.6V cordless drill needs recharging. By the time I'm finished drilling, I also need recharging.

CHAPTER 4

Pollination

• •

Super Pollinator - Where's the fruit?

T he *Mason bee* is the best fruit pollinator around, but is only active during April, May and part of June. The types of produce usually blooming at that time are apple, plum, cherry, pear and almond trees as well as some strawberries and blueberries. Check out your garden and note the types of plants blooming in this time period. Remember fruit blossoms last about a week. This means that other flowers must be blooming in the interim so that the bee can continue to have nourishment during its adult life cycle with the end result of having more Mason bees for next year. By having extra Mason bees, I can distribute (in bamboo tubes, straws or cocoons) them to friends and acquaintances.

The Mason bee can outpollinate the honeybee at about an 80 to 1 ratio. Each bee type has her own special landing approach to the flower. The bees' descent upon the flower ensures pollination. However, there is a tremendous difference in how much pollination occurs at that one encounter. Think of the Mason bee as doing a belly flop onto the flower. The numerous hairs (scopa) on her body allow some of the pollen to stick to her abdomen. Her actions literally knock the pollen grains off their anther (the male portion) and sends them onto the stigma column. The pollen travels down the tube to the ovary where fertilization takes place. See *Figure 4.1*.

The honeybee appears to be very demure and collects pollen very carefully. Her objective is to collect pollen on her pollen baskets located on the rear legs - the tibia. She approaches the flower at one side of the base and works

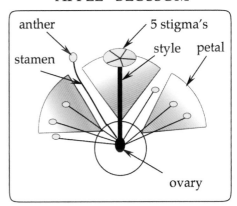

APPLE BLOSSOM

anther   5 stigma's

stamen   style   petal

ovary

Figure 4.1

her way in. In fact she may not even touch the anther. She'll have to make at least 80 more trips to match her Mason bee counterpart. Pollen collecting results in about 15-20 trips a day for the Mason bee, but it is the amount that is collected each time that is significant. Your season's yield will indeed be abundant.

If you have fruit trees, using Mason bees will result in more fruit because of their exemplary ability to pollinate. For example, it takes about 250 Mason bees to pollinate one acre of apple trees and 20,000 honeybees to do the same job. In backyard-gardener statistics that would be about 2 to 4 female Mason bees and 160 to 320 honeybees for each tree. As is typical of the bee society, the female is the pollinator. Her active adult life is about 8 to 10 weeks. In between the fruit tree blooming cycles she will find alternative flower provisions. See *Figure 4.2.*

The bees don't always follow scientific data and though the life cycle typically ends in June, I have noticed a few females surviving into July. The males who serve primarily as drones for about 2 weeks, can sometimes still be found hanging around after 3 weeks. The window of opportunity to mate no longer exists as the females are busy performing their motherly duties which do not include any further relationship with the male. The bees' life cycle will sometimes be moved out if spring-like weather is delayed.

Figure 4.2 - Mason bee enjoying a Rhododendron

I, personally, do not have an acre of apple trees, but I do have 3 different types of apple trees, along with two cherry trees, a peach tree, two pear trees, two plum trees and some blueberry bushes. I continue to add to my "orchard" so that I can experiment and take full advantage of my Mason bees. *Figure 4.3* depicts our Newtown Pippin apple tree from the blossoming period to full fruit production over a 4-month time span.

It is commonplace to associate only the honeybee with the pollination process. It is well-known that they have become a commercialized business. Their hives are transported great distances from state to state. Because of CCD (Colony Collapse Disorder), people are more aware than ever of the seriousness of the situation and want to know how they can help. The media coverage on this crisis is creating more of a concern about how we are affecting our environment. There are several factors being addressed and it looks to be the "perfect storm" - in other words, numerous exact conditions

Newtown Pippin + Female Mason Bee

April 29th   August 26th

+ =

Figure 4.3

(not desirous) come together to cause their destruction. The honeybee has indeed become susceptible to many negative outside influences, including stress, viruses and mites.

The wild honeybees are in worst shape. According to the latest statistics, 90% of their populations have been annihilated. The human race has taken away their habitat through rural expansion, chemical additives and of course, just plain, simple ignorance of preserving the natural world about them.

Our wild (native) Mason bee is one of the best hopes for pollination. So, if you have a couple of fruit trees or berry bushes, then the Mason bee is the way to go. Whatever you've got to offer, she'll pollinate for you.

CHAPTER 5

Housing

• •

Assisted Living

There are several options in providing a nesting unit for your Mason bees. The care and management of these bees is easy and fun to do.

In this chapter, I start with the "Basic Nesting Block" and proceed to using bamboo reeds - "The Bamboo Bungalow." The idea of building a "basic nesting block" is still very popular, but I do see a trend towards trays and "canned bees." Canned bees consist of a can filled with tubes or straws and sometimes bees are part of the package deal; they are being sold as a unit to help people get started with using Mason bees for their pollinating needs. On the other hand, the nesting block - in my opinion - is like an old fashion log cabin home with a bit of nostalgic appeal.

Nesting trays (*Figure 5.1*) are some of the more "advanced" technologies used in harvesting cocoons in the fall (See **Chapter 8 - Preparing and Storing Cocoons**). The trays have interlocked sections that separate for cleaning and easy removal of cocoons. These units can be purchased in plastic or wood. Of course, you do have the option of building your own trays. See *Project 5* - Stacking Trays.

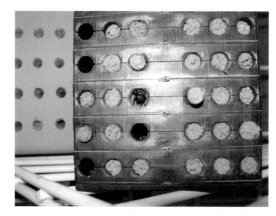

Figure 5.1 - Nesting trays in foreground & Nesting block in background

> **Note:** Nesting units are also called "traps." I prefer not to use this term. In my opinion, the word "trap" implies a killing device instead of a home or shelter.

No matter what your housing preference might be, the goal is to provide a home for our native bees. If you have wood posts on hand, just start drilling holes. Later, you can experiment and try other methods until you figure out just exactly what you want to do. A unit of 25 - 50 holes is more than sufficient for the average backyard gardener.

Just about anything that has about a 5/16th-inch hole is attractive to Mason bees. Of course they don't always follow this rule of thumb and you may find the bees occupying holes anywhere from 1/4-inch up to 1/2-inch.

The Cliff Dwellings

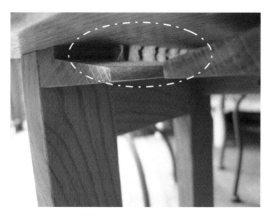

Figure 5.2 - The Cliff Dwelling

A very unique construction project occurred under a small table that I had on my balcony. The Mason bees created their own cliff dwellings (*Figure 5.2*). They chose to build mud walls against an angled wood support along one length of a small table that I had on my balcony.

This little bee is very creative and focused in her quest to find a home for her future children. In fact, if I happen to be in her path, she buzzes about my head, investigating the possibility of using either my nostrils or ears as nesting holes. I gently wave my hand to discourage her and step to one side to let her proceed to any of the housing units that I've provided for her.

Location, Location, Location

Locate the nesting units facing east or southeast so that they will began warming up early in the day. The bees do not have the ability to heat themselves, so the sooner they get that morning sun, the sooner they'll get started pollinating your crops. This early start allows them more time for foraging and creating cells for their eggs.

It is important to provide a sheltered area to protect the unit from all types of weather. Shelter ideas include a balcony, patio umbrella, a rural mailbox and wooden boxes... to name a few. By using a plastic pipe shelter (See *Figure 5.3*), the nesting unit is easy to locate near the fruit trees that need to be pollinated. My wine rack (*Figure 5.4*) is another idea of using smaller plastic pipe combined with bundled bamboo reeds. I usually place the wine rack in an area where I can observe the bees on a regular basis.

Figure 5.3

Once you've placed the unit securely in a particular area, **do not move** it until the holes are filled. The bee has a built-in GPS (Global Positioning System) to determine the coordinates of the hole that she is working on. If the nest is moved, it is lost and gone as far as she is concerned and she will not be able to find it even if it is moved only a couple of feet from the original position. If the unit is moved only a few feet from its first location, she will repeatedly investigate and fly about the original sight with much bewilderment. Once all the holes have been filled, you can replace it with another unit.

Figure 5.4 - The Wine Rack Unit

If you feed squirrels or birds, be sure to locate the bee nesting units away from that area. Birds sometimes peck open the mud plugs and squirrels may toss straws or bamboo sticks on the ground.

The Mud

The bee needs a mud source to complete the seal on the cell. She will search until she finds an area that contains wet clay soil (*Figure 5.5*). The area shown is at the base of one of our embankments that is consistently wet because of the underground springs that we have.

The bees have their own formula for determining the moisture content of the soil that is

Figure 5.5

Figure 5.6

Figure 5.7

needed to form a wall for the cell. She will dig until she reaches the right balance of moisture-to-soil content. To help with the excavation process, I poke holes into the soil with a stick or wooden dowel. The bee then uses her own tools (mandibles) to create a ball of mud and carry it back to the cell. After about 10 - 12 trips she will have collected enough material to fully complete the masonry of the cell.

Figure 5.6 shows the bee putting on the final plug which has a bit of rough texture to it. At this point she has sealed several cells and this plug - the final seal of the entrance - will be a lot thicker (about 1/4 inch). *Figure 5.7* shows not only the final plug, but also reveals the Mason bee's tenacious effort to seal the area between the outside of the straw and the inner portion of the bamboo reed. Initially when I placed the straw in the bamboo, I left an extension for easy removal. It's obvious that the bee was not aware of my plans.

Creating a Mud Reserve

In the past I have attempted to set up a mud reserve by providing a dish of moist soil near the nesting shelter. However, my endeavors were ignored. If, on the other hand, you feel it imperative to create a special mudded patch, locate it in the garden near (25 - 50 feet) the nesting site, and keep it evenly moist. Dig out an area as if you were planting a shrub, but do not use potting soil, sand or gravel as these types of soil dressings won't be the correct consistency for the bee to create her masonry. Use clay/mineral type soil that is natural to your area. Creating this reserve may save your bees extra time and energy in searching for mud resources.

Other Homesteaders

Your bee sanctuary might become a hostel for similar solitary bees and maybe a wasp or two. I find it interesting to observe these outsiders as well. You may feel it necessary to create additional housing with different size holes to accommodate everyone.

 Hint: *Plastic straws may hold moisture and cause cell to mold. Too much moisture is an ideal breeding situation for mites as well.*

•The Basic Nesting Block - (*Project 1*)

For a quick start, I use a two 2" x 4's" screwed or nailed together, about 10 - 12 inches long, and drill 5/16-inch holes that are 3-1/2 nches deep (the length of my drill bit). A hole depth of 6 inches provides room for a few more female bees - here you would have to use a longer bit and more wood. If you wish to use straw liners (See *Project 4* for making your own), then you'll need to drill the holes a little larger in diameter to accommodate the liners. For mounting purposes attach a 1/2" x 1" strip of wood that extends above and below the block.

•The Shelter and Bee Stick Assembly - (*Project 2*)

The plastic pipe shelter with either bundled straws or bamboo reeds provides a nest protected from the weather.

•The Bamboo Bungalow - (*Project 3*)

Cut bamboo reeds in 6-8 inch lengths and bundle. With some of the larger bamboo reeds, I insert straws (store-bought or my own homemade ones).

•Straws - (*Project 4*)

This project uses parchment paper. It is moisture resistant and makes a very nice and strong straw. For winter harvesting of the cocoons, you just cut the tape and unroll the cocoons.

•Trays - (*Project 5*)

Trays can be purchased from a supplier or you can make your own. The trays are another method for easy cocoon harvesting. My illustration on the project page is a springboard design to get you started.

The Basic Nesting Block

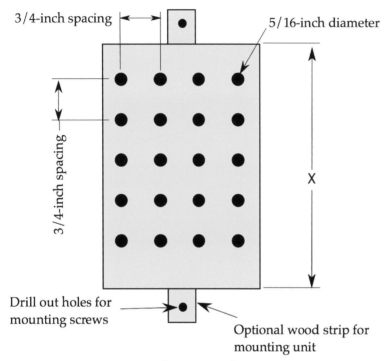

3/4-inch spacing

5/16-inch diameter

3/4-inch spacing

X

Drill out holes for
mounting screws

Optional wood strip for
mounting unit

1. Use a 6" x 6" or a 4" x 4" (or 2-2"x4's") block of wood. Cut to any desired 'X' length.

2. Mark face of block with 3/4" x 3/4" grid. Use 1/8 drill bit to create pilot holes.

3. Use 5/16 drill bit to create nesting holes. A "brad" bit creates smooth holes, but is on the expensive side. If using straw liners, use 3/8 drill bit. Don't drill through.

4. Use a rat-tail file or rotate a pencil inside the hole and edges to smooth it out. Tap block (face down) to clean out sawdust.

Hint: As I drill, I "pump" the drill bit in and out, cleaning out the sawdust as I penetrate the wood.

The Shelter and Bee Stick Assembly

This bee stick is designed to fit into a 2-inch PVC pipe.

Materials:

- (1) Washer: 1/2-inch I.D. x 2-inch O.D.
- (1) 1/2-inch wooden dowel, 10 inches long
- Electrician's tape or masking tape
- 10-inches PVC Pipe
- 2-inch PVC cap

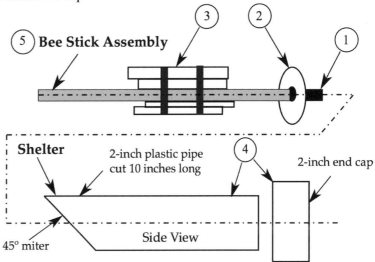

5 **Bee Stick Assembly**

Shelter

2-inch plastic pipe
cut 10 inches long

2-inch end cap

45° miter

Side View

1. Wrap end of dowel a couple of times with tape (3/4-inch area). Create enough thickness to keep washer from slipping off.

2. Slip washer over untaped end, slide along dowel, and force fit onto the tape. This should secure it and keep washer from slipping off.

3. Arrange bamboo or tubes around the dowel. Use rubberbands to hold together.

4. Push end cap onto pipe to create shelter unit.

5. Slide in the Bee Stick Assembly.

Hint: Be sure the 2-inch washer clears the inside of the 2-inch plastic pipe. Some pipes have a thicker wall. If so, use 1-1/2-inch washer.

The Bamboo Bungalow

1.   Select bamboo with approximately 5/16 inch to 3/8 inch inside diameter.

2.   Cut lengths from 5 - 7 inches. .

3.   Tie or rubber band 5 - 6 bamboo sticks into a bundle and place in a protected area, keeping bamboo in horizontal position. Bundle can also be placed in an open can or box. (Example: Use a 1-qt. or 1/2 gal. milk/juice carton for housing the sticks; I've also used cookie cans, coffee cans and plastic beverage containers.)

4.   Bundle around the "Bee Stick Assembly" and place in a 2-inch plastic pipe and with a 2-inch end cap. **See *Project 2*.**

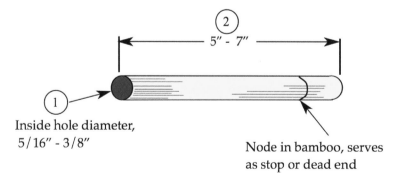

② 5" - 7"

① Inside hole diameter,
5/16" - 3/8"

Node in bamboo, serves
as stop or dead end

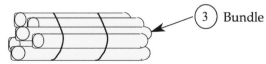

③ Bundle

Hint: Insert straw liners into the bamboo. When iner is filled it can be replaced with new one.

Straws/Liners

Materials: parchment paper, tape, wooden pencil

1.   Cut 5- inch width of parchment and cut into thirds.

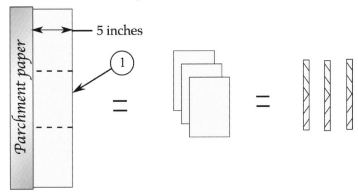

2.   Using pencil, roll paper, from point "A" to point "B", tucking the triangle end of point "A" and rolling to point "B".

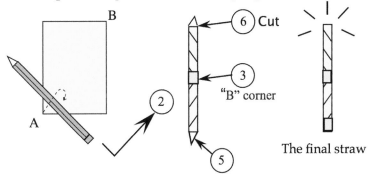

The final straw

3.   Wrap tape around entire straw to secure the end at point "B."

4.   Remove pencil.

Hint: Parchment paper (found in the baking section of the grocery store) makes the straws water resistant.

5.   Fold over one end of straw and wrap with tape.

6.   Cut off opposite end so that straw is 5 or 6 inches in length.

Stacking Trays

Materials: wood (scrap 1 x 6's), 4 bolts, 4 nuts, 4 washers, and 4 wood screws

Tools: drill, router or gouging tool, rattail file

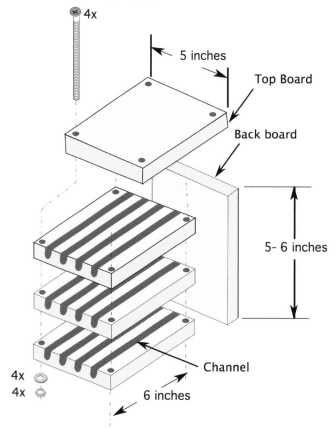

1. Cut 4 trays. (3 trays will have channels) and route channels (Use router or gouging tool) full length, 3/8-inch wide and 3/8 inch deep.

2. Use a rattail file or sandpaper to smooth out the channels.

3. Add top cover, bolt trays together and attach the unit with wood screws to the back board.

CHAPTER 6
Food Sources

• •

Eat, Drink and be Merry

Flowers provide two life-sustaining properties: nectar and pollen. The nectar (flower juice) is an essential nutrient for the adult bees, but it is also the binding agent for bee bread. The bee bread is comprised of pollen - the dry ingredient- and nectar - the wet ingredient - and is placed in the cell as provisions for the future larva.

Fruit tree flowers alone may not provide enough nourishment for your bees. Blooms last less than two weeks for each type of tree. The bee will need nourishment between and after blooming periods to continue laying her eggs and setting up each cell's provisions.

Your particular microclimate will determine the blooming cycles for your area. This is the time to record such time periods. Write it down either on a calendar or in a garden diary. One shrub, in particular, that I found blooming early in the

Figure 6.1 - Andromeda

season was the Andromeda (*pieris japonica*). This is an easy to maintain no-brainer shrub to have growing on your property. *Figure 6.1* is a picture of an Andromeda that I have in a large pot on my balcony. It is located near my Mason bees' housing units. It is loaded with bell-shaped flower clusters and is a favorite for the bees. This particular plant is always ready to provide the male bee with immediate sustenance (energy nectar) so that he will be ready to take on courtship. The Andromeda also acts as an interim provider of nectar during the bee's nest-building period.

Favorite Colors

A bee's favorite colors are found in the ultraviolet range. It is good to note that red is not part of this spectrum though we know it to be a hummingbird attraction.

Listed below, by their common names, are some of the flowers, trees, fruits and shrubs that are blooming during the Mason bee's active adult cycle. A consolidated plant list is shown within the petal that best represents its flower color.

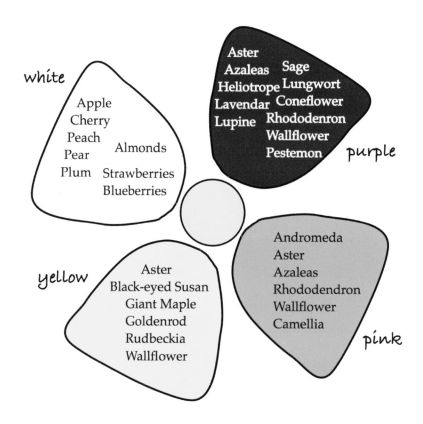

white

Apple
Cherry
Peach
Pear   Almonds
Plum   Strawberries
  Blueberries

purple

Aster
Azaleas   Sage
Heliotrope   Lungwort
Lavendar   Coneflower
Lupine   Rhododenron
  Wallflower
  Pestemon

yellow

Aster
Black-eyed Susan
Giant Maple
Goldenrod
Rudbeckia
Wallflower

pink

Andromeda
Aster
Azaleas
Rhododendron
Wallflower
Camellia

Hint: *Hybridized and double-blossom flowers do not offer enough nourishment for the bees.*

Native flowers are less maintenance, but the bee won't mind if you interlace your garden with some nonnative favorites.

In *Figure 6.2* is a female Mason bee enjoying some Heliotrope. I found this to be another favorite for the bees and for me as well. It's fragrance reminds me of the soft smell of baby powder. The bottom line is that the bees really go for it.

Remember if we provide food for the bees, they, in turn, will provide for us.

Figure 6.2

CHAPTER 7

Life Cycle

· ·

*T*he *numerical sequence* shown on this chart coincides with the order of information contained in this chapter.

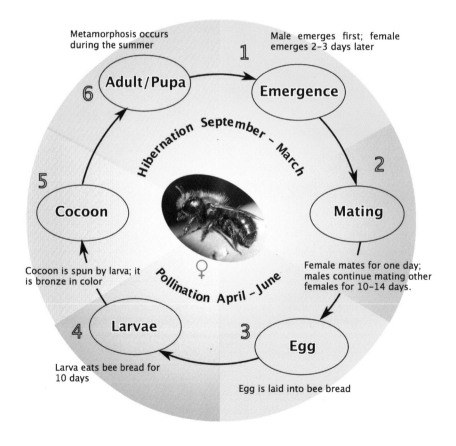

Metamorphosis occurs during the summer

Male emerges first; female emerges 2–3 days later

1   **Emergence**

6   **Adult/Pupa**

Hibernation September – March

2   **Mating**

5   **Cocoon**

♀

Pollination April – June

Female mates for one day; males continue mating other females for 10–14 days.

Cocoon is spun by larva; it is bronze in color

4   **Larvae**

3   **Egg**

Larva eats bee bread for 10 days

Egg is laid into bee bread

Emergence

When the temperature reaches 50°F, the bees wake up. However, they prefer temperatures of 55°F - 60°F to go out and about. This temperature/time frame can be anywhere from the end of February to the end of March. The weather is not always predictable and sometimes correct flying temperatures

Figure 7.1 - Bee emerging from cocoon

don't occur until April.

The male bee is the first to make an appearance. *Figure 7.1* depicts a full adult male Mason bee emerging from his cocoon. In *Figure 7.2* we see a male emerging from a mudded plug that was created in a wooden nesting

Figure 7.2 - Male bee emerging through a mud plug

block. Depending on temperatures, the female will usually follow in 2 - 3 days. If you happen to miss seeing the bees emerge, just look near the nesting hole. One of the first things that the bee does when he emerges is poops (defecates). It tends to look like cream-colored or light brown paint specks. The female, on the other hand, doesn't get much of a chance to do anything because the males are pouncing on her.

Figure 7.3 - Male Mason bee

Figure 7.3 shows a full bodied male who has more of a green iridescent sheen than the more common blue-black description given to the Blue Orchard Bee (Osmia Lignaria). The temperature was about 50°F and he wasn't moving much so I had an opportunity to take his picture. After the photo session I placed him near a bamboo reed and he walked in and waited for things to warm up. Male bees do

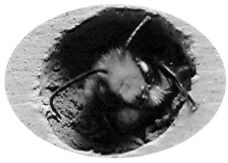

Figure 7.4 - Female Mason bee

not have stingers or any apparatus to defend themselves. They are totally harmless; their goal in life is to just charm the ladies.

Figure 7.4 shows the female, stout-bodied and with mandibles. She's ready to create mud balls for her future masonry work on the chamber walls of each nursery. Although she is equipped with a stinger, it is only used for emergency defense situations.

Mating

At the first sign of spring when the temperatures are about 55°F, the male is the first to emerge. He is sexually mature and not quite sure what to do with himself. He pounces on just about anything that moves, including other males and sometimes other insects such as the Box Elder Beetle. The female

usually makes her debut a few days later. In the meantime the male needs to maintain energy and will partake of nectar from nearby flowers. Once the female appears, the males seem to find their purpose in life and jump on her before she even gets a chance to dry her wings. *Figure 7.5* shows a male on the back of a female as she clings to the bamboo reed from which she had just emerged. Normally I fine mating masses on the ground. There will often be several males piled on top of each other - sometimes in opposite directions - with a single female underneath it all.

After the female has experienced a form of speed dating, she's now starts preparing for motherhood which includes creating a nest and gathering food for her future larvae.

Figure 7.5 - Mason bees mating

Egg

When she selects her first nesting hole, she uses her unique pheromone to provide a scent identity which usually deters other females from entering her nesting cavity.

It is estimated that the female Mason bee lays about 30 - 35 eggs during her short life span. Egg production is contingent upon the weather. If there are too many cold days (temperatures below

50°F), her body will use the unused egg material as sustenance. The egg is not a type that hatches, but instead, evolves into a larva.

Figure 7.6 shows a clear tube in which one can see the cell chambers (walls of mud) that house the individual larvae-to-be. The cells are about 5/8th of an inch long. When the female lays her egg, she backs into the tube and positions herself so that the egg sticks right into the middle of the bee bread. This way her baby has immediate access to food.

Illustration of cells

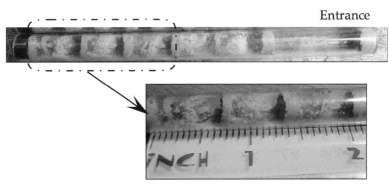

Entrance

Figure 7.6

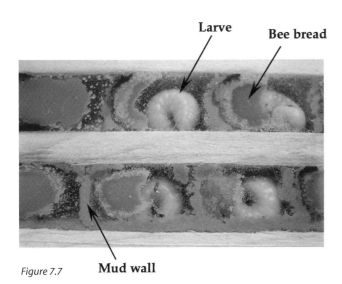

Larve

Bee bread

Figure 7.7   **Mud wall**

Larvae

Within 3 days the larva reveals itself with fine segmentation. It is pearly white in appearance and moves ever so slightly. Like any newborn, it conserves its actions to eating and pooping. Its feces appear as dark granules surrounding its body (*Figure 7.7*)

Cocoons

Although my emphasis is basically a labor-free method of rearing Mason bees, I will cover some of the steps that can be taken to rescue the cocoons from mites. If you are looking to pollinate some acreage, you might want to consider the harvesting method.

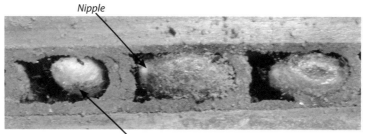

Nipple

Figure 7.8   Larva starting to spin

Figure 7.8 depicts some cocoons in an open observation box. The cocoons are a glazed honey-nut color with a thin opalescent membrane.. Note the larva on the left is just starting to spin. All the bee bread is now gone. The middle and right cells show the "cocooning" process is just about complete. There is a "nipple" formed on one end of the cocoon; this is the end from which the bee will emerge. Over time the cocoons will become darker and more bronze to brownish (*Figure 7.9*).

Figure 7.9

Adult/Pupa

By fall a full adult bee has formed. Metamorphosis is complete. If you have chosen to harvest the cocoons , this is the time to do it. See **Chapter 8 - Winterizing Bees.**

CHAPTER 8
Winterizing Bees

• •

Bedding down for Winter

Fall is my favorite time of year. The weather is cool and invigorating. I like the idea of getting ready for winter: mulching the ground, prepping some plants and most of all checking on my Mason bees.

Here are a couple of different approaches to take when winterizing the Mason bees.

Method I: No Work . . . almost

Method I relies on the balance of nature. You can literally leave the Mason bees in their current location. However, be sure that they are protected from the impending winter rains and snow. The key is to keep the nesting unit dry. Cold temperatures are not an issue - remember these are native bees; their genus extends clear up into Canada. All you have to remember is that about the 1st of March you'll need an additional housing unit to accommodate the next generation. You'll also find that some of the bees will prefer to do their own housecleaning (*Figure 8.1*) and will reuse their previous bungalow. In the upper right-hand corner you can see a couple of Mason bees pushing out debris.

Depending on the location

Figure 8.1 - Housecleaning

of your units you might want to add a screen covering to prevent invaders from destroying the cocoons. I've also used old pantyhose to pull over my housing blocks. If you do relocate the units, do not store in an area that will reach temperatures of 50ºF or more. Otherwise, you may have bees emerging sooner than expected.

I've used an old bookcase to arrange some of my basic block units as well as plastic shoe boxes stored with straws and bamboo reeds. The clear plastic boxes serve as a visual reminder. We have a roof overhang on our balcony that protects my projects from getting wet. I finalize my winter preparation by covering the front of the bookcase with an old window screen

Method II: Cocoon Preparation

The month of October is the most ideal time to partake in a different sort of harvest - the harvesting of cocoons. If you have used straws or trays, now is the time to inspect and clean the cocoons and prepare them for the early spring.

WORK AREA

First set up a work area. This is the one time you can bring your bees indoors and work comfortably at room temperature. The bees are not ready to emerge as yet and the short time needed to prepare the cocoons will not affect them. Use a table or countertop to lay out your materials. Locate yourself near a water source for the cocoon washing process. I use my kitchen. My husband is very careful about what he snacks on during this period of time, especially since the drying cocoons look a bit like honey-glazed peanuts or one of my organic experiments.

Materials: plastic tablecloth, old toothbrush, one-gallon plastic bucket, paper towels, slotted spoon, containers to separate the cocoon (styrofoam meat trays, muffin tins, lids or ?)

EXTRACTING THE COCOONS

- **Nesting Trays**

    If you used nesting trays, now is the time to separate them and remove the cocoons. I've used anything from a fingernail file to a popcicle stick to gently lift or push the cocoon loose from the canal. You also have the option of purchasing a special cocoon scoop from either an on-line supplier, nursery or local Mason bee supplier.

- **Straws/Liners**

    Cardboard tubes (guards) have liners that can be removed. You can use a pair of tweezers to grasp the mud plug end and pull the liner from the tube. If the tube looks to be in good shape, you can use it again next year. If the plug becomes damaged, it doesn't matter because you're taking the straw apart any way. Not to worry. No harm will come to the bee as it is still safely in its cocoon. You can cut the straw liner very carefully with an exacto knife. My homemade straws (See *Project 4* in **Chapter 5 - Housing**) can be easily unrolled by removing the taped tab.

INSPECTING THE COCOONS

This method is extremely important for determining not only how many cocoons you have, but it is also an excellent way to check for mites and other infestations such as moth larvae and carpet beetle larvae which will do considerable damage to the cocoons. Also look for holes in the cocoons. These signs are definite indicators that a

Figure 8.2 - Cocoons before washing

parasite has taken over. I have found as many as 12 Monodontomerus wasps in one cocoon. If I find anything questionable, I put the cocoons in a separate disposable container so as not to contaminate the strong healthy ones. Also at this time, you can count and see how many male and female cocoons you have. The female cocoons will be slightly larger.

WASHING THE COCOONS

I use a one gallon plastic bucket and fill with tepid water. I put the cocoons in the water and gently churn the water to release mud and feces. Next I take each cocoon and gently brush off debris with a soft toothbrush. I choose to use clear water only. In *Figure 8.3*

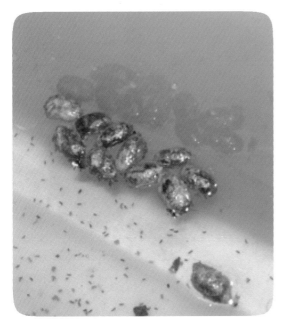

Figure 8.3 - Cocoon pontoons

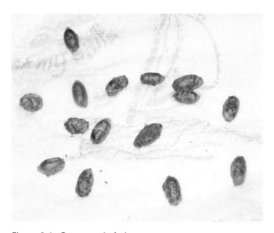

Figure 8.4 - Cocoons air drying

you will notice that the cocoons look like little pontoons floating on the surface of the water.

DRYING COCOONS

After cleaning the cocoons in the water, I lift them out with a slotted spoon and lay them on paper towels to dry. I gently roll each cocoon on the paper towel to remove excess moisture. Next I lay the cocoons on fresh paper towels and let air dry overnight (*Figure 8.4*).

STORING THE COCOONS

The next day put the cocoons in a container with a lid. I've used clean peanut or almond cans (which are really heavy cardboard tubing) with their own plastic lids. I mark the outside of the can with a label: "Mason bee cocoons - open in March" I also cut a hole (about 1/2-inch diameter) on the side for them to use as the escape hatch. To reuse the cans for next year, just plug the hole with a cork. With the plastic lid you can lift it to take a peek off and on to see how they're doing.

Mark the Calendar

Mark your calendar for next year so that you don't forget your locked up bees. Start observing the weather patterns and temperatures about the first part of March. If temperatures seem to be warming up too soon (50°F +) for 3 - 4 days in a row, and you don't have a food source (blossoms) for your bees, you might want to consider storing them in a refrigerator - **not the freezer** - until you have flowers available. Do not think you can store your bees longer than their intended cycle. Even in the cold storage of a refrigerator, they have been known to emerge.

Also during this time check out where you would like to locate your bee shelter or nesting unit. If you have only one unit, consider building or adding a second unit for the emerging bees.

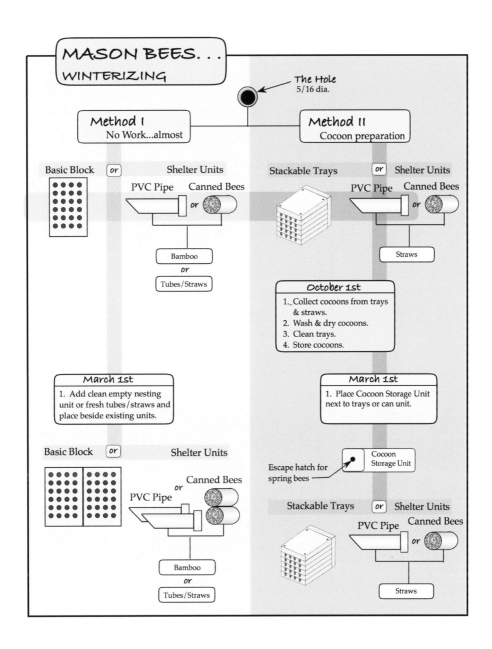

MASON BEES. . .
WINTERIZING

The Hole
5/16 dia.

Method I
No Work...almost

Method II
Cocoon preparation

Basic Block or

Shelter Units

PVC Pipe   Canned Bees

or

Bamboo
or
Tubes/Straws

Stackable Trays or Shelter Units

PVC Pipe   Canned Bees

or

Straws

October 1st
1. Collect cocoons from trays
   & straws.
2. Wash & dry cocoons.
3. Clean trays.
4. Store cocoons.

March 1st
1. Add clean empty nesting
unit or fresh tubes/straws and
place beside existing units.

March 1st
1. Place Cocoon Storage Unit
next to trays or can unit.

Basic Block or

Shelter Units

Canned Bees

or

PVC Pipe

Bamboo
or
Tubes/Straws

Escape hatch for
spring bees

Cocoon
Storage Unit

Stackable Trays or Shelter Units

PVC Pipe   Canned Bees

or

Straws

CHAPTER 9
Enemies

• •

The *Mason bee* faces many perils in her struggle to survive . In this chapter I feature the key predators that I've encountered and offer solutions or alternative methods of preventing future infestations or destruction to your Mason bees.

Mites

Although the Mason bee is immune from the varroa and tracheal mites that infect honeybees, they are not without mites. The particular specie of mites that affect Mason Bees is called Kromein's hairy-footed mite (Chaetodactylus Krombeini) - believe it or not it is a native parasite. They look like reddish sand particles sprinkled on the bee's back (thorax & abdomen sections). *Figure 9.1* is a photo of a male Mason bee infested with mites. In this particular case, the bee was still able to fly but not very well. These mites are at a stage of their life cycle that they do not feed on the adult bee because they do not have a mouth. However, they can restrict the bee's ability to fly and thus still end up killing it by preventing it from getting to a food source. The mite's offspring can take over a cell by consuming bee bread and the larva or egg.

Figure 9.2 depicts a cell that has been infested with mites. The food provision has become a fluffy yellow pile of loose granulated pollen mixture. The original thick bee bread has become puff pastry.

The mites will hang out in a cell until the bee emerges from its cocoon. The female

Figure 9.1 - Male Mason bee with mites

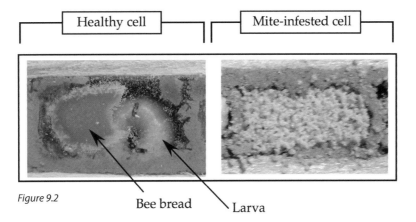

Figure 9.2   Bee bread   Larva

mites have claws and attach themselves to not only the bee within the chamber but any bee passing through during its emergence.

Mites like cold, damp wood and can thrive from season to season in the basic bee block. One can try to dry out the block using low oven temperatures; just be sure there are no bees occupying some of the drilled out sites. Using bleach or any other type of chemical to clean the block will defeat the purpose of caring for these bees. In the past, I did use a little bleach in water to clean a block and the bees waited 2 years before they would use it again. Using Method II - Chapter 8 allows inspection of cocoons and helps break up the mites' life cycle.

Using straws or liners can help with the hygiene of the nesting block, but the liners can have their own set of problems such as carpet beetles and the mon-odontomerus wasps.

Ovipositor

Figure 9.3

Parasitic Wasps

In this chapter I'll only be talking about the Monodonto-merus wasp because it is the one that I've had personal experience with and I found it the most detrimental. It is a small (about 1/4-inch long) parasitic wasp that lays its eggs in the Mason bee's cocoon. In June the wasps appear in small swarms. They are looking to inject their ovipositor into the freshly spun cocoon of a Mason bee larva. It is amazing how these wasps know the larvae locations. *Figure 9.3* shows the wasp's profile and *Figure 9.4* a wasp searching a bamboo reed for larvae location.

Protecting Mason bee nesting units by June 1st will prevent some wasp infestation. You can cover your units with fine mesh wire or a pair of old pantyhose. The wasps have easiest access to the seams of trays and front mud entrances. This is also the time to collect straws and cardboard tubes and place then in an enclosed container for storage. *Figure 9.5* shows infestation by these wasps in one of my plastic tray units. This is one time I had not put the trays in a safe place and the end results were not good.

Figure 9.4

Figure 9.5

Figure 9.6

Figure 9.7

Carpet Beetles

There are a variety of carpet beetles. They are well known in museums for damaging paperwork and insect specimens. *Figure 9.6* is a photograph of one of the larva that I found in my straws. This larva was about 3/8-inches long and *Figure 9.7* shows its path of destruction to one of my straws.

Pesticides

When it comes to using pesticides - I just don't, but I'm not a commercial grower and don't have any obligations to any criteria outside my own environment. If one has fruit trees, usually the dormant sprays are applied before blooms appear. During the dormant season I find that I'm just too dormant myself to go outside and apply the spray. Once the tree starts blooming, do not use any type of chemical that would leave residue on the blossoms. Even fertilizers can be harmful. If you have sprayed in and around your fruit trees, be sure to remove surrounding vegetation that might be contaminated. This cleanup is not only good for the bees, but also for you, your family and pets. There is a lot of information available for old fashioned alternatives so why not give them a try.

The Bee Fly

The bee fly is another predator that I encountered in my garden early in the spring. It was hanging upside down on a branch. This photograph is a view of its underside (*Figure 9.8*). It is a superficial bee. It looks for opportunity to lay its eggs in the Mason bee's nest. The bee fly larvae then eat the Mason bee

Figure 9.8 - Bee Fly

larvae. There's not much you can do to prevent this event from happening. Standing by the nesting site with a fly swatter is just too time-consuming.

Birds

It is best not to feed birds near the nesting sites. Of course, it doesn't keep them from from searching for the larvae. They will eagerly peck out the mud plugs on Mason bee units, trying to access this food source. The larger the bird, the more damage that is possible to the nesting unit. *Figure 9.9* is an example of a wooden nesting unit that was attacked by a Pile-ated Woodpecker.

To prevent this type of destruction one could use a wire basket, hung upside down and over the wooden block. The idea is to block any bird from pecking out the holes or even destroying the entire nesting unit.

Figure 9.9

Figure 9.10 – Photo by Robert G. New

Squirrels

(Figure 9.10)

Even these cute little acrobats of the woods, town and country can be harmful to Mason bees. I've found bamboo tubes and straws scattered all over my balcony. These are usually the tubes that I've placed loosely in an open rural mailbox. Once I bind the tubes and place in a PVC shelter, the squirrels seem to lose interest.

Buzz Words

Anther: the portion of the stamen where pollen is produced.

Bee bread: a mixture of pollen and nectar used as food by the larvae of the bees.

Carpenter Bee: A solitary bee that excavates holes in wood.

Cell: the space division created by the female bee for the larva to grow.

Crop specific: Usually said of honeybees. For example, honeybees may be dedicated to pollinate one specific crop.

Honey: a product created by the honeybee, using nectar and pollen.

Hive: usually a man-made housing unit for honeybees.

Larva (p. larvae): the 2nd stage of metamorphosis.

Mandibles: mouth parts used as cutting tools and to create mud pellets.

Mason Bee: A common name for our solitary bee (genus osmia); she derives her name from the fact that she uses mud and earth elements to seal her cells.

Metamorphosis: the process of transformation from egg to adult bee.

Nectar: the sweet liquid in a flower that provides energy and food for bees and other insects.

Nesting box: a housing unit to provide a space for the bee to complete its metamorphisis.

Pheromone: female bee scent that allows her to mark her territory as well as attract males.

Pollen: yellow powdery substance found on male stamen to fertilize the ovaries of a flower.

Pollination: the process that completes the fertilization process to produce fruit.

Pupa: the 3rd stage of metamorphosis.

Queen: the female bee that produces eggs.

Scoba: The small brushlike tuft of hairs.

Social bee: an organized family structure with a division of labor that serves a single queen bee.

Solitary bee: a bee that is her own queen bee and creates the provisions for one egg at a time.

Stamen: The male portion of a flower with pollen grains.

Stigma: The female portion of a flower in which pollen grains are received to eventually fertilize the flower.

Straw liners: These are tubes made of a special plastic-coated paper. Homemade version is either freezer paper or baking parchment.

Tubes: These are cardboard tubes, usually 4 mil thick that have straw liners.

Thorax: the middle section of an insect that has wings, legs and most of its muscles.

Other Sources

· ·

Books:

1. "The Orchard Mason Bee" by Brian L. Griffin
2. "Pollination with Mason Bees" by Dr. Margriet Dogsterom
3. "Mason-Bees" by Henry Fabre; copyright 1916
4. "New Biology" by W. M. Smallwood, Ida L. Reveley & Guy A. Bailey; copyright 1924

Here are some favorite links that include suppliers and informational sources. I am not associated, nor do I endorse the following products. I only list them as a possible source in obtaining Mason bee supplies

Suppliers:

Backyard Bird Shop: http://www.backyardbirdshop.com
This store carries solitary bee houses, straws and liners. They are also a source for purchasing cocoons early in the year.

BeeDiverse Products: http://www.beediverse.com
This is a Canadian-based company headed up by Dr. Margriet Dogsterom (author of "Pollination with Mason Bees"); they provide various Mason bee supplies and cocoons. Their specialty are stackable plastic-type tray units that are easy to clean for cocoon harvesting. They also have kid activity kits.

Knox Cellars: http://www.knoxcellars.com
This company was started by Brian Griffin (author of "The Orchard Mason Bee"). He has since

"retired" but his family continues the tradition of providing solitary bee supplies. I have also seen their supplies available locally.

Pollinator Paradise: http://www.pollinatorparadise.com

Dr. Karen Strickler is the owner of Pollinator Paradise. Her company offers bee management systems (Binderboards®). There are a variety of package deals: a Garden package, a Beginner Small Orchard package and on up to a Professional package. Each package contains an equal number of male and female bees. Both the Blue Orchard bees (*Osmia lignaria*) and the Hornfaced bees (*Osmia cornifrons*) are sold.

Territorial Seed Co: http://www.territorialseedcompany.com

This company provides Mason bees and supplies.

Favorite Websites:

Colorado State University

Leafcutter Bees: http://www.ext.colostate.edu/pubs/insect/05576.html

Pollinator's Paradise: http://www.pollinatorparadise.com

This site is packed with information on almost any kind of pollinating insect: solitary bees, wasps, etc.

Washington State University

http://gardening.wsu.edu/library/inse006/inse006.htm

Xerces Society: http://www.xerces.org

This group has helped me identify insects. I've taken pictures with my digital camera and emailed them; in turn, they have emailed the pertinent information for identification.

Other Articles:

Increase Pollination With Mason Bees

Author: Susan Ward
Pub: May 28, 2002
URL: http://www.suite101.com/article.cfm/3319/92210

How to Raise and Manage Orchard Mason Bees for the Home Garden
    Author: Stephen Bambara, Extension Entomologist
    Pub: By NC Cooperative Extension
    URL: http://www.ces.ncsu.edu/depts/ent/notes/Other/note109/note109.html

Screening to keep out tiny Monodontomerus wasp parasites
    http://www.pollinatorparadise.com

Suggested Plants for Native Bees
    http://www.attra.org/attra-pub/nativebee.html

Beetools (Mason Bees) by Ron Bennett
    http://members.aol.com/beetools/mason.htm

CPSIA information can be obtained at www.ICGtesting.com
Printed in the USA
BVIW12n0009210115
384210BV00003B/9